FIRE YOUR JOB
HIRE
YOUR
PASSION
Journal

Billy F. Wroe Jr.

ISBN: 978-1-0879-2815-9 (paperback)
ISBN: 978-1-08802-475-1 (hardcover)

www.1stWroe.com

Welcome to
Your Passion Journal!

Welcome to the *Fire Your Job, Hire Your Passion Journal!* If you are reading this, you have made a great decision to fully invest in your experience by documenting your journey. The wonderful thing about journals is that they give us the ability to look back on our thoughts from the perspective of where we were mentally at their point of origin. This journal was design to capture the essence of your experiences both inside and outside of the reading. In addition, by providing a dedicated space to complete exercises, it encourages accountability. Within this tool you will find the following:

- **Chapter Reviews**
- **Passion Point Journal Pages**
- **Timeout Exercise Worksheets**
- **Free Flow Journal Pages**
- **Success Schedules (Chapter 7)**
- **3 Exclusive Exercises**
  - **What's Happening Journal Pages (All Chapters x 2)**
  - **The Wisdom Quadrant (Chapter 10)**
  - **Take a Moment Section Reviews**

There is no way that you can complete this journal without being changed by the end. In the beginning, writing your thoughts and insights might be a struggle, but stick with it. Over time, even if the amount of words does not increase, you will find yourself intentionally thinking deeper about your experiences. I encourage you to explore everything that those depths have to offer. Share your experiences throughout your journey on social media by using the #FYJHYP. Each time that you do share your experience you will be creating a timestamp for you to use later as the years progress. Before I ask you to make your commitment to this process, I want to share some inspiration about your greatness to get you started. It is time to put in the work that both you and your passion are worthy of!

I Believe You Are Great

I believe you are great. That you were specifically chosen for this very moment because there is a purpose for your life. I am sure that you have been through failures. I know that you have experienced pain, but that was just to develop you. To strengthen your ability to endure through adversity when others would simply turn and walk away. From their passion. From their hopes. From their desire to experience the life that for so long they have only been able to taste with their eyes closed. Not you. You are not willing to settle because you know that you deserve success. You've been replaying it over and over in your mind since you were a child. Working night and day to perfect your craft, knowing that anyone successful had to pick their face up out of the dirt at least once or twice in their lifetime. What they focused on was the lesson. One more check off the list on how to do it wrong, while their passion ignites the fuse for the next attempt to get it right.

See, there will come a time when you will have to fight. You will have to push yourself harder, think faster, hold yourself to a higher standard and dig in so you can stand your ground against the opponents of your vision. I am not talking about those on the outside who would rather see you fail with them than succeed without them. I am talking about the mindset of doubt that cripples the very foundation of what you already know to be true. Zig Ziglar referred to it as False Evidence Appearing Real. F.E.A.R. of success presents no case, yet still, we give it place. When all it does is take up our time in this space.

No one's compass points to mediocrity. Many people want what others have worked to accomplish but are too busy taking pictures in the mirror instead of mirroring the same disciplines that have been proven to produce the results that they say they seek. If you want something different than what you have, you have to be willing to do something that you have never done. If you want something that no one has ever had, you have to focus on innovation rather than imitation. So what will you do? I ask, if you are who you are today because of who you practiced being yesterday, then who are you practicing to be for tomorrow?

Rather than doubt yourself and the possibilities, I challenge you to doubt impossibility. I already know that you are great because greatness is in each and every one of us. Waiting for us to grab hold of it. To develop it. To nurture it. To embrace everything that this life is meant to be with it. If nobody else does, I believe in you. I can believe in you because I found the courage to believe in myself. The only question left is…

What do you believe?

~Billy F. Wroe Jr.

The Top 5

What are your
top 5 Reasons for
reading this book?

{
1. _____
2. _____
3. _____
4. _____
5. _____
}

Make a commitment

_____   _____

Signature   Date

THE LAYOFFS

Sometimes the best thing that can happen in our life is an intentional layoff.

Chapter 1 Review

You Have a Job to do

Date

Chapter Started: _____

Chapter Completed: _____

What information in the chapter
resonated with you?

Pages to revisit:

- Page:____
- Page:____
- Page:____
- Page:____
- Page:____
- Page:____
- Page:____
- Page:____

What are 3 insights that you learned or rediscovered about yourself?

Inspired Thoughts

_____

_____

_____

_____

_____

_____

_____

_____

_____

_____

_____

_____

_____

_____

_____

_____

_____

_____

_____

_____

_____

_____

_____

BILLY F. WROE JR.

What's Happening?

Date: _____

What opportunities have you had to put into practice the information from this chapter? How have you been able to manifest your preferred outcome?

_____

_____

_____

_____

_____

_____

_____

_____

_____

_____

_____

_____

_____

_____

_____

_____

_____

_____

What's Happening?

Date: _____

What opportunities have you had to put into practice the information from this chapter? How have you been able to manifest your preferred outcome?

_____

_____

_____

_____

_____

_____

_____

_____

_____

_____

_____

_____

_____

_____

_____

_____

_____

_____

Free Flow Journal

Date: _____
Prompt: _____

_____

_____

_____

_____

_____

_____

_____

_____

_____

_____

_____

_____

_____

_____

_____

_____

_____

_____

_____

_____

_____

_____

Free Flow Journal

Date: _____
Prompt: _____

_____

_____

_____

_____

_____

_____

_____

_____

_____

_____

_____

_____

_____

_____

_____

_____

_____

_____

_____

_____

_____

Timeout (Net Worth)

Take a moment to ask yourself the following 2 questions. You may need to do some research to determine your answers.

- ○ Is your net worth positive or negative?
  - **Net worth:** Value of all of your Assets minus all of your Debts.

- ○ Can you afford to take 2 weeks off unpaid and dedicate that time to invest in something you are passionate about?

Asset Descriptions

- **Cash** - Money available in bank accounts
- **Property** - Value of real estate or land owned
- **Personal Property** - Vehicles, jewelry, or other tangible items of value
- **Investments** - Stocks, bonds, certificate deposits, or other items that take time to liquidate.

Debt Descriptions

- **Loans** - Auto loans, mortgage, or personal loans
- **Credit Cards** - Any unsecured debt

Net Worth

Assets	Value
Cash	$
Property	$
Personal Property	$
Investments	$
Total Assets	**$**

Debts	Balance
Loans	$
Credit Cards	$
Total Debts	**$**

Total Assets	$
- Total	$
Net Worth	**$**

What is your largest asset?

_____

What is your largest debt?

_____

Monthly Budget

Unpaid Time Off	
Total Monthly Bills	$
Monthly Bills ÷ 2	$
Savings	$
Savings - (Monthly Bills ÷ 2)	**$**

*If your final number is negative, taking 2 weeks off unpaid would cause a financial hardship. How can you fix or improve this equation?

BILLY F. WROE JR.

Passion Point (Your Story)

What is the "Once upon a time" story that guides your financial discipline?
- I don't know about investing.
- I don't make enough money.
- I can't afford to save.

_____

_____

_____

_____

_____

_____

_____

_____

_____

_____

_____

_____

_____

_____

_____

_____

Passion Point (Missed Opportunities)

How many opportunities have you missed because of a lack of preparation?

Which one is most recent?

How can you prepare today if it were to come back around?

_____

_____

_____

_____

_____

_____

_____

_____

_____

_____

_____

_____

_____

_____

_____

_____

BILLY F. WROE JR.

Timeout (Time Travel)

If you need, close your eyes to help immerse yourself in the experience? Grab a single piece of paper. Take a moment to feel the texture of the paper as you hold it in your hands. Now set the paper down and visualize yourself ripping that piece of paper into 4 pieces. Really imagine what that process would be like. Hear the paper's sound as it tears, feel the vibration on your fingertips as you separate each piece, see what each piece looks like after you are done making 4 pieces. Visualize that for about 10 seconds. Now open your eyes and tear the piece of paper into the 4 pieces that you imagined. Write one of the following four words on each piece of paper. "Time Travel Does Exist." Save the 4 pieces of paper in your passion journal or in your book. What just happened?

How can you use visualization to your advantage?

_____

_____

_____

_____

_____

_____

_____

_____

_____

There is no limit to where you can travel to in your time machine. Go everywhere that you want to visit, and be intentional about the details.

Passion Point (Making a Connection)

How do you connect to the present?

_____

_____

_____

_____

_____

_____

_____

_____

_____

_____

_____

_____

_____

_____

_____

_____

_____

_____

_____

_____

Chapter 2 Review

Just Enough Isn't Enough

Date

Chapter Started: _____

Chapter Completed: _____

What information in the chapter
resonated with you?

Pages to revisit:

- Page:____
- Page:____
- Page:____
- Page:____
- Page:____
- Page:____
- Page:____
- Page:____

What are 3 insights that you learned or rediscovered about yourself?

Inspired Thoughts

BILLY F. WROE JR.

What's Happening?

Date: _____

What opportunities have you had to put into practice the information from this chapter? How have you been able to manifest your preferred outcome?

_____

_____

_____

_____

_____

_____

_____

_____

_____

_____

_____

_____

_____

_____

_____

_____

_____

_____

What's Happening?

Date: _____

What opportunities have you had to put into practice the information from this chapter? How have you been able to manifest your preferred outcome?

_____

_____

_____

_____

_____

_____

_____

_____

_____

_____

_____

_____

_____

_____

_____

_____

BILLY F. WROE JR.

Free Flow Journal

Date: _____
Prompt: _____

_____

_____

_____

_____

_____

_____

_____

_____

_____

_____

_____

_____

_____

_____

_____

_____

_____

_____

_____

_____

_____

Free Flow Journal

Date: _____
Prompt: _____

_____

_____

_____

_____

_____

_____

_____

_____

_____

_____

_____

_____

_____

_____

_____

_____

_____

_____

_____

_____

_____

_____

Timeout (Stack Ranking)

Instructions

Think about the team you are working on right now. If the team has 100's of people, dwindle that number down to your immediate sphere with a maximum of 12 coworkers (be sure to include yourself). Beginning with the number 1 (highest importance), stack rank each team member. Write notes as to how you decided to prioritize each individual. Remember, this is not a popularity contest, but solely about the perceived value of each individual as they correspond to the company. It is ok to be brutally honest.

Once you have every team member ranked, divide the total team count by 3. Round that result up to the next whole number (ex. if you have 7 team members your result would be 3) and place a red X by the name of that many of the lowest ranked employees. Take the next lowest ranked employees and place a circle next to the name of that many employees. At this point only the top employees should not have anything next to their names.

Where did you fall in the list? What was next to your name? Those names with a red X are the employees that would have the highest probability for termination if the company decided to execute a layoff tomorrow. The employees with the circle next to their name are on the bubble. These employees could possibly be terminated or keep their job, depending on how much money the company is attempting to save. Lastly, there are the employees that have nothing next to their names. Though these employees are not on the bubble, even they can be in jeopardy of termination, under the right set of unfortunate circumstances.

Now look at your rank and determine if that is where you wanted to be. Would you even have a chance at retaining your job? Do you have the potential to score even higher? What can you do to challenge yourself at your current level? Take these insights and write out some goals to improve your rank in one specific way before your next evaluation.

Though you are measuring yourself against others, always remember that you are your competition. You are attempting to outdo you, and sometimes out doing others happens to be a byproduct of that activity. You can do this exercise with any group of people that you engage with, it does not have to only apply to the work environment. As you improve your value, revisit this exercise often to measure your progress.

Timeout (Stack Ranking)

Rank 1
Name:
Rank Reason:

Rank 2
Name:
Rank Reason:

Rank 3
Name:
Rank Reason:

Rank 4
Name:
Rank Reason:

Rank 5
Name:
Rank Reason:

Rank 6
Name:
Rank Reason:

Rank 7
Name:
Rank Reason:

Rank 8
Name:
Rank Reason:

Rank 9
Name:
Rank Reason:

Rank 10
Name:
Rank Reason:

Rank 11
Name:
Rank Reason:

Rank 12
Name:
Rank Reason:

Insights
What can you do to challenge yourself at your current rank?
What do you need to do to improve your rank?

Passion Point (Daily Challenges)

What areas are you challenging yourself to grow in daily?

_____

_____

_____

_____

_____

_____

_____

_____

_____

_____

_____

_____

_____

_____

_____

_____

_____

_____

_____

_____

BILLY F. WROE JR.

Chapter 3 Review

Time is of the Essence

Date

Chapter Started: _____

Chapter Completed: _____

What information in the chapter
resonated with you?

Pages to revisit:

- Page:____
- Page:____
- Page:____
- Page:____
- Page:____
- Page:____
- Page:____
- Page:____

What are 3 insights that you learned or rediscovered about yourself?

Inspired Thoughts

_____

_____

_____

_____

_____

_____

_____

_____

_____

_____

_____

_____

_____

_____

_____

_____

_____

_____

_____

_____

_____

_____

_____

BILLY F. WROE JR.

What's Happening?

Date: _____

What opportunities have you had to put into practice the information from this chapter? How have you been able to manifest your preferred outcome?

_____

_____

_____

_____

_____

_____

_____

_____

_____

_____

_____

_____

_____

_____

_____

_____

_____

_____

What's Happening?

Date: _____

What opportunities have you had to put into practice the information from this chapter? How have you been able to manifest your preferred outcome?

_____

_____

_____

_____

_____

_____

_____

_____

_____

_____

_____

_____

_____

_____

_____

_____

BILLY F. WROE JR.

Free Flow Journal

Date: _____
Prompt: _____

_____

_____

_____

_____

_____

_____

_____

_____

_____

_____

_____

_____

_____

_____

_____

_____

_____

_____

_____

_____

_____

_____

Free Flow Journal

Date: _____

Prompt: _____

_____

_____

_____

_____

_____

_____

_____

_____

_____

_____

_____

_____

_____

_____

_____

_____

_____

_____

_____

_____

_____

BILLY F. WROE JR.

Passion Point (Invested Time)

What is a worthy investment of your time?

What do you get in return for investing that time?

_____

_____

_____

_____

_____

_____

_____

_____

_____

_____

_____

_____

_____

_____

_____

_____

_____

_____

_____

Passion Point (Piroritization)

What do you consider to be the highest priority in your life right now?

_____

_____

_____

_____

_____

_____

_____

_____

_____

_____

_____

_____

_____

_____

_____

_____

_____

_____

_____

Chapter 4 Review

Dreams Are Supposed to Live Outside of the Box

Date

Chapter Started: _____

Chapter Completed: _____

What information in the chapter
resonated with you?

Pages to revisit:

- Page:____
- Page:____
- Page:____
- Page:____
- Page:____
- Page:____
- Page:____
- Page:____

What are 3 insights that you learned or rediscovered about yourself?

Inspired Thoughts

_____

_____

_____

_____

_____

_____

_____

_____

_____

_____

_____

_____

_____

_____

_____

_____

_____

_____

_____

_____

_____

_____

BILLY F. WROE JR.

What's Happening?

Date: _____

What opportunities have you had to put into practice the information from this chapter? How have you been able to manifest your preferred outcome?

_____

_____

_____

_____

_____

_____

_____

_____

_____

_____

_____

_____

_____

_____

_____

_____

_____

_____

What's Happening?

Date: _____

What opportunities have you had to put into practice the information from this chapter? How have you been able to manifest your preferred outcome?

_____

_____

_____

_____

_____

_____

_____

_____

_____

_____

_____

_____

_____

_____

_____

_____

_____

BILLY F. WROE JR.

Free Flow Journal

Date: _____
Prompt: _____

_____

_____

_____

_____

_____

_____

_____

_____

_____

_____

_____

_____

_____

_____

_____

_____

_____

_____

_____

_____

_____

_____

Free Flow Journal

Date: _____
Prompt: _____

_____

_____

_____

_____

_____

_____

_____

_____

_____

_____

_____

_____

_____

_____

_____

_____

_____

_____

_____

_____

_____

Timeout (Failure Opportunities)

Take a moment to write down four of your most recently experienced failures. For this exercise, it does not matter whether the failures were public or private. Select one failure from the list to perform a deep dive on. What were some of the warning signs that presented prior to the failure occurring? Were there any warning signs that you chose to ignore or not take seriously? Get intimate with the opportunities you had to either avoid the failures or at least speed up the failure process. If you cannot identify opportunities, what did you learn from the failures? I am not referring to the heightened emotionally-compromised lessons, but the healthy tools you gained from the experiences. In this exercise, really attempt to separate the fat from the meat. Write down each insight that you are able to identify. You are going to use these insights to develop a strategy designed to intentionally disrupt the loop between your actions, failures, and lessons. This is a living list that will grow as you experience new failures and gain additional insights throughout your life, so keep them in a place where they will be readily available.

Failures {
_____
_____
_____
_____

Failure:	Warning Signs:
Missed Opportunities:	**Insights:**

Failure:	Warning Signs:
Missed Opportunities:	**Insights:**

BILLY F. WROE JR.

Take a Moment (The Layoffs)

Before we transition to The Interviews section, take a moment to reflect on your journey thru The Layoffs. Which job mentality did you struggle with the most going in? What do you feel was the foundation of those struggles? How can you appreciate yourself for sticking with your commitment? Answer these questions with as many one-word responses that you can. Then using those answers create a gratitude statement that acknowledges wisdom learned and refreshed.

Which job mentality did you struggle with most? Why?

What can you appreciate about making this journey?

Write a gratitude statement that encompasses that journey.

_____

_____

_____

_____

THE INTERVIEWS

An interview is nothing more than
an opportunity to learn about
something new.

Chapter 5 Review

Your Passion has an Identity

Date

Chapter Started: _____

Chapter Completed: _____

What information in the chapter
resonated with you?

Pages to revisit:

- Page:____
- Page:____
- Page:____
- Page:____
- Page:____
- Page:____
- Page:____
- Page:____

What are 3 insights that you learned or rediscovered about yourself?

Inspired Thoughts

_____

_____

_____

_____

_____

_____

_____

_____

_____

_____

_____

_____

_____

_____

_____

_____

_____

_____

_____

_____

_____

_____

_____

What's Happening?

Date: _____

What opportunities have you had to put into practice the information from this chapter? How have you been able to manifest your preferred outcome?

_____

_____

_____

_____

_____

_____

_____

_____

_____

_____

_____

_____

_____

_____

_____

_____

_____

_____

Free Flow Journal

Date: _____
Prompt: _____

_____
_____
_____
_____
_____
_____
_____
_____
_____
_____
_____
_____
_____
_____
_____
_____
_____
_____
_____
_____
_____
_____
_____

BILLY F. WROE JR.

Free Flow Journal

Date: _____
Prompt: _____

_____

_____

_____

_____

_____

_____

_____

_____

_____

_____

_____

_____

_____

_____

_____

_____

_____

_____

_____

Passion Identity Tool

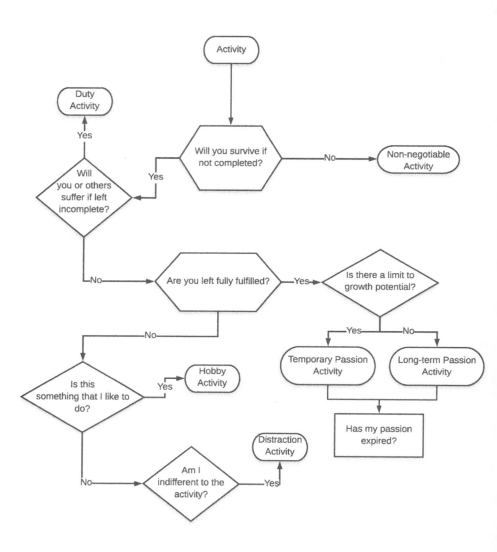

BILLY F. WROE JR.

Passion Point (Passion Identity)

Your passions do not have to be larger than life activities. Passions can be found in the simplicity of a flower or the rage of the sea.

What are some of the smaller passions that you have that fly under the radar?

_____

_____

_____

_____

_____

_____

_____

_____

_____

_____

_____

_____

_____

_____

_____

_____

_____

Passion Point (Hobby Passions)

One person's passion can be another person's hobby and vice versa. Be careful not to adopt the emotions of others as your own for the activities that you engage in.

Have any hobbies infiltrated your passions?

_____

_____

_____

_____

_____

_____

_____

_____

_____

_____

_____

_____

_____

_____

_____

_____

_____

BILLY F. WROE JR.

Timeout (Passion ID Practice)

Take a moment to review the Passion ID Tool categories. Now, using the activity that you are currently engaged in (reading) let's determine how that corresponds to your passion identity. It is not about how what you are reading resonates with you, but the purpose of what the activity of reading is to you that matters. These are the questions I would like you to ask yourself about reading. Once you answer yes to one of the questions, stop and dig deeper.

- If you do not read, will you die?
  Dig Deeper
    a) What will cause the death?

- If you do not read, will you or others suffer as a result?
  Dig Deeper
    a) What is the source of the suffering?
    b) Who suffers directly and/or indirectly?

- Does reading fulfill you?
  Dig Deeper
    a) What emotions/feelings are encompassed in the complexity of fulfillment?
    b) Is there a limitation to the fulfillment?

- Is reading something that you like to do?
  Dig Deeper
    a) What enjoyment do you get from the activity?

- Are you indifferent to reading?
  Dig Deeper
    a) Why do you choose this activity to preoccupy your time?

b) Is there something else that you could do that would be more meaningful to you?

What type of activity was reading (Circle one)?

Non Negotiables   Duties   Passions   Hobbies   Distractions

What did digging deeper reveal?

BILLY F. WROE JR.

Chapter 6 Review

Feel, Think, Passion

<u>Date</u>

Chapter Started: _____

Chapter Completed: _____

What information in the chapter
resonated with you?

Pages to revisit:

- Page:____
- Page:____
- Page:____
- Page:____
- Page:____
- Page:____
- Page:____
- Page:____

What are 3 insights that you learned or rediscovered about yourself?

Inspired Thoughts

BILLY F. WROE JR.

What's Happening?

Date: _____

What opportunities have you had to put into practice the information from this chapter? How have you been able to manifest your preferred outcome?

_____

_____

_____

_____

_____

_____

_____

_____

_____

_____

_____

_____

_____

_____

_____

_____

_____

_____

What's Happening?

Date: _____

What opportunities have you had to put into practice the information from this chapter? How have you been able to manifest your preferred outcome?

_____

_____

_____

_____

_____

_____

_____

_____

_____

_____

_____

_____

_____

_____

_____

_____

_____

_____

BILLY F. WROE JR.

Free Flow Journal

Date: _____
Prompt: _____

_____

_____

_____

_____

_____

_____

_____

_____

_____

_____

_____

_____

_____

_____

_____

_____

_____

_____

_____

_____

_____

_____

_____

Free Flow Journal

Date: _____
Prompt: _____

_____
_____
_____
_____
_____
_____
_____
_____
_____
_____
_____
_____
_____
_____
_____
_____
_____
_____
_____
_____
_____
_____

BILLY F. WROE JR.

Timeout (Emotional Check-in)

Take a moment to replay your day. What emotional events have you felt thus far? Did you gloss over the events, or did you stop to engage with them? If you chose to engage with your emotions, did you do so in a healthy manner?

Emotional Event 1

Emotion (Circle one): **Happy   Sad   Fear   Anger   Shame   Other:** _____

Event: _____
_____
_____
_____
_____
_____

Interaction (Circle one): **Ignore   Engage**

Outcome of engagement: _____
_____
_____
_____
_____
_____

Emotional Event 2

Emotion (Circle one): **Happy   Sad   Fear   Anger   Shame   Other:** _____

Event: _____
_____
_____
_____
_____

Interaction (Circle one): **Ignore   Engage**

Outcome of engagement: _____
_____
_____
_____
_____

Emotional Event 3

Emotion (Circle one): **Happy   Sad   Fear   Anger   Shame   Other:** _____

Event: _____
_____
_____
_____
_____

Interaction (Circle one): **Ignore   Engage**

Outcome of engagement: _____
_____
_____
_____
_____

Passion Point (Surrendering to Fear)

How many times have you allowed yourself to quit something that you are passionate about due to fear? How many more times are you going to allow this to be acceptable?

_____

_____

_____

_____

_____

_____

_____

_____

_____

_____

_____

_____

_____

_____

_____

_____

_____

_____

_____

Passion Point (Default Emotions)

What is the default emotion that you tend to rely on more than others?

_____

_____

_____

_____

_____

_____

_____

_____

_____

_____

_____

_____

_____

_____

_____

_____

_____

_____

_____

_____

BILLY F. WROE JR.

Chapter 7 Review

Developing Your Passion

Date

Chapter Started: _____

Chapter Completed: _____

What information in the chapter
resonated with you?

Pages to revisit:

- Page:____
- Page:____
- Page:____
- Page:____
- Page:____
- Page:____
- Page:____
- Page:____

What are 3 insights that you learned or rediscovered about yourself?

Inspired Thoughts

_____

_____

_____

_____

_____

_____

_____

_____

_____

_____

_____

_____

_____

_____

_____

_____

_____

_____

_____

_____

_____

_____

_____

BILLY F. WROE JR.

What's Happening?

Date: _____

What opportunities have you had to put into practice the information from this chapter? How have you been able to manifest your preferred outcome?

_____

_____

_____

_____

_____

_____

_____

_____

_____

_____

_____

_____

_____

_____

_____

_____

_____

_____

What's Happening?

Date: _____

What opportunities have you had to put into practice the information from this chapter? How have you been able to manifest your preferred outcome?

_____

_____

_____

_____

_____

_____

_____

_____

_____

_____

_____

_____

_____

_____

_____

_____

_____

Free Flow Journal

Date: _____
Prompt: _____

_____

_____

_____

_____

_____

_____

_____

_____

_____

_____

_____

_____

_____

_____

_____

_____

_____

_____

_____

_____

Free Flow Journal

Date: _____
Prompt: _____

_____
_____
_____
_____
_____
_____
_____
_____
_____
_____
_____
_____
_____
_____
_____
_____
_____
_____
_____
_____
_____
_____
_____

BILLY F. WROE JR.

Success Schedule (Instructions)

Instructions

Phase 1:

The success schedule tool uses a simple tracking spreadsheet to break down the entire week hour by hour, 24 hours a day. In the first phase (about a 2-week period) it allows the user to document each hour of their current routine. Each item has a category that it falls into; sleeping, eating/cooking, working, grooming, family time, personal development, social media time, phone time, etc. At the end of each day the number of hours spent in each category are tallied and should equal 24 hours.

Phase 2:

The second phase of the success schedule process is probably the most tedious. In this phase, we are asked to write out the number of hours we want to allocate to each category daily. This number does not have to be uniform. Each day is treated individually and can consist of whatever the desire is for that specific day. For instance, maybe Monday, Tuesday, Thursday, and Friday you want to get 6 hours of sleep, but on Wednesday, Saturday, and Sunday you want to get 7 hours. Once we have the desired hours allocated, we look at the variance between that and the results from the phase 1 success schedules. This allows us to visualize how far off we are from where we want to be. We then take the responsibilities that cannot be moved such as work and plug them into the success schedule for the upcoming week. Thus begins the negotiation of priorities.

Phase 3:

The third phase 3 of the success schedule process is ongoing. Not in the sense of forever, but until we develop a new autopilot program that gets us the better results that we seek, we will have to repeat this exercise weekly. In this phase we write out our success schedule, predetermine what we are going to do with our leftover time, and outside of an emergency, we stick to the plan.

Success Schedule (Phase 1)

SUCCESS SCHEDULE - WEEK 1								
	MON	TUE	WED	THURS	FRI	SAT	SUN	
0:00								0:00
1:00								1:00
2:00								2:00
3:00								3:00
4:00								4:00
5:00								5:00
6:00								6:00
7:00								7:00
8:00								8:00
9:00								9:00
10:00								10:00
11:00								11:00
12:00								12:00
13:00								13:00
14:00								14:00
15:00								15:00
16:00								16:00
17:00								17:00
18:00								18:00
19:00								19:00
20:00								20:00
21:00								21:00
22:00								22:00
23:00								23:00

Success Schedule (Phase 1)

Date: /   /   **Current Routine**

	MON	TUE	WED	THURS	FRI	SAT	SUN	
				SUCCESS SCHEDULE - WEEK 2				
0:00								0:00
1:00								1:00
2:00								2:00
3:00								3:00
4:00								4:00
5:00								5:00
6:00								6:00
7:00								7:00
8:00								8:00
9:00								9:00
10:00								10:00
11:00								11:00
12:00								12:00
13:00								13:00
14:00								14:00
15:00								15:00
16:00								16:00
17:00								17:00
18:00								18:00
19:00								19:00
20:00								20:00
21:00								21:00
22:00								22:00
23:00								23:00

Success Schedule (Phase 1 Review)

Phase 1: Week 1

PRIORITIES	SUCCESS IS MY DUTY							TOTALS
WORK								
PERSONAL								
EAT								
SLEEP								
TOTALS:								

Phase 1: Week 2

PRIORITIES	SUCCESS IS MY DUTY						TOTALS
WORK							
PERSONAL							
EAT							
SLEEP							
TOTALS:							

Which priorities took up the majority of your weeks?

_____

_____

_____

_____

Success Schedule (Phase 2)

Date: /   /   Ideal Routine

	MON	TUE	WED	THURS	FRI	SAT	SUN	
SUCCESS SCHEDULE								
0:00								0:00
1:00								1:00
2:00								2:00
3:00								3:00
4:00								4:00
5:00								5:00
6:00								6:00
7:00								7:00
8:00								8:00
9:00								9:00
10:00								10:00
11:00								11:00
12:00								12:00
13:00								13:00
14:00								14:00
15:00								15:00
16:00								16:00
17:00								17:00
18:00								18:00
19:00								19:00
20:00								20:00
21:00								21:00
22:00								22:00
23:00								23:00

Success Schedule (Ideal vs. Autopilot)

Phase 2: Ideal Routine

PRIORITIES	SUCCESS IS MY DUTY							TOTALS
WORK								
PERSONAL								
EAT								
SLEEP								
TOTALS:								

How far off were the first 2 weeks in phase 1 from your ideal routine? What activities took you off track?

_____

_____

_____

_____

How can you be more focused in the upcoming week?

_____

_____

_____

_____

What one activity do you want to commit your leftover time to in the upcoming week?

_____

_____

Success Schedule (Phase 2)

Date: / /   Planned Routine

	MON	TUE	WED	THURS	FRI	SAT	SUN	
			SUCCESS SCHEDULE - WEEK 1					
0:00								0:00
1:00								1:00
2:00								2:00
3:00								3:00
4:00								4:00
5:00								5:00
6:00								6:00
7:00								7:00
8:00								8:00
9:00								9:00
10:00								10:00
11:00								11:00
12:00								12:00
13:00								13:00
14:00								14:00
15:00								15:00
16:00								16:00
17:00								17:00
18:00								18:00
19:00								19:00
20:00								20:00
21:00								21:00
22:00								22:00
23:00								23:00

Success Schedule (Planned vs. Ideal)

Phase 2: Planned Routine (Week 1)

PRIORITIES	SUCCESS IS MY DUTY							TOTALS
WORK								
PERSONAL								
EAT								
SLEEP								
TOTALS:								

How far off was week 1 in phase 2 from your ideal routine? What activities took you off track?

_____

_____

_____

Did you use your leftover time as you planned? How can you be more focused in the upcoming week?

_____

_____

_____

What one activity do you want to commit your leftover time to in the upcoming week?

_____

_____

Success Schedule (Phase 2)

Date: / /   **Planned Routine**

	MON	TUE	WED	THURS	FRI	SAT	SUN	
0:00								0:00
1:00								1:00
2:00								2:00
3:00								3:00
4:00								4:00
5:00								5:00
6:00								6:00
7:00								7:00
8:00								8:00
9:00								9:00
10:00								10:00
11:00								11:00
12:00								12:00
13:00								13:00
14:00								14:00
15:00								15:00
16:00								16:00
17:00								17:00
18:00								18:00
19:00								19:00
20:00								20:00
21:00								21:00
22:00								22:00
23:00								23:00

SUCCESS SCHEDULE - WEEK 2

Success Schedule (Planned vs. Ideal)

Phase 2: Planned Routine (Week 2)

PRIORITIES	SUCCESS IS MY DUTY							TOTALS
WORK								
PERSONAL								
EAT								
SLEEP								
TOTALS:								

How far off was week 2 in phase 2 from your ideal routine? What activities took you off track?

_____

_____

_____

Did you use your leftover time as you planned? How can you be more focused in the upcoming week?

_____

_____

_____

What one activity do you want to commit your leftover time to in the upcoming week?

_____

_____

Success Schedule (Phase 2)

Date: /   /   Planned Routine

	MON	TUE	WED	THURS	FRI	SAT	SUN	
SUCCESS SCHEDULE - WEEK 3									
0:00									0:00
1:00									1:00
2:00									2:00
3:00									3:00
4:00									4:00
5:00									5:00
6:00									6:00
7:00									7:00
8:00									8:00
9:00									9:00
10:00									10:00
11:00									11:00
12:00									12:00
13:00									13:00
14:00									14:00
15:00									15:00
16:00									16:00
17:00									17:00
18:00									18:00
19:00									19:00
20:00									20:00
21:00									21:00
22:00									22:00
23:00									23:00

Success Schedule (Planned vs. Ideal)

Phase 2: Planned Routine (Week 3)

PRIORITIES	SUCCESS IS MY DUTY							TOTALS
WORK								
PERSONAL								
EAT								
SLEEP								
TOTALS:								

How far off was week 3 in phase 2 from your ideal routine? What activities took you off track?

_____

_____

_____

Did you use your leftover time as you planned? How can you be more focused in the upcoming week?

_____

_____

_____

What one activity do you want to commit your leftover time to in the upcoming week?

_____

_____

Success Schedule (Phase 2)

	MON	TUE	WED	THURS	FRI	SAT	SUN	
SUCCESS SCHEDULE - WEEK 4								
0:00								0:00
1:00								1:00
2:00								2:00
3:00								3:00
4:00								4:00
5:00								5:00
6:00								6:00
7:00								7:00
8:00								8:00
9:00								9:00
10:00								10:00
11:00								11:00
12:00								12:00
13:00								13:00
14:00								14:00
15:00								15:00
16:00								16:00
17:00								17:00
18:00								18:00
19:00								19:00
20:00								20:00
21:00								21:00
22:00								22:00
23:00								23:00

Success Schedule (Planned vs. Ideal)

Phase 2: Planned Routine (Week 4)

PRIORITIES	SUCCESS IS MY DUTY							TOTALS
WORK								
PERSONAL								
EAT								
SLEEP								
TOTALS:								

How far off was week 4 in phase 2 from your ideal routine? Did an emergency take you off track?

_____

_____

_____

Did you use your leftover time as you planned? How can you be more focused in the upcoming week?

_____

_____

_____

What one activity do you want to commit your leftover time to in the upcoming week?

_____

_____

Success Schedule (Phase 3)

Date: / /   **Committed Routine**

	MON	TUE	WED	THURS	FRI	SAT	SUN	
SUCCESS SCHEDULE - WEEK 1								
0:00								0:00
1:00								1:00
2:00								2:00
3:00								3:00
4:00								4:00
5:00								5:00
6:00								6:00
7:00								7:00
8:00								8:00
9:00								9:00
10:00								10:00
11:00								11:00
12:00								12:00
13:00								13:00
14:00								14:00
15:00								15:00
16:00								16:00
17:00								17:00
18:00								18:00
19:00								19:00
20:00								20:00
21:00								21:00
22:00								22:00
23:00								23:00

Success Schedule

(Committed vs. Emergency)

Phase 3: Committed Routine (Week 1)

PRIORITIES	SUCCESS IS MY DUTY							TOTALS
WORK								
PERSONAL								
EAT								
SLEEP								
TOTALS:								

Did you keep all of your commitments? What took you off track?

_____

_____

_____

Did you use your leftover time as you planned? How can you be more focused in the upcoming week?

_____

_____

_____

What one activity do you want to commit your leftover time to in the upcoming week?

_____

_____

Success Schedule (Phase 3)

Date: / /   **Committed Routine**

	MON	TUE	WED	THURS	FRI	SAT	SUN	
SUCCESS SCHEDULE - WEEK 2								
0:00								0:00
1:00								1:00
2:00								2:00
3:00								3:00
4:00								4:00
5:00								5:00
6:00								6:00
7:00								7:00
8:00								8:00
9:00								9:00
10:00								10:00
11:00								11:00
12:00								12:00
13:00								13:00
14:00								14:00
15:00								15:00
16:00								16:00
17:00								17:00
18:00								18:00
19:00								19:00
20:00								20:00
21:00								21:00
22:00								22:00
23:00								23:00

BILLY F. WROE JR.

Success Schedule

(Committed vs. Emergency)

Phase 3: Committed Routine (Week 2)

PRIORITIES	SUCCESS IS MY DUTY							TOTALS
WORK								
PERSONAL								
EAT								
SLEEP								
TOTALS:								

Did you keep all of your commitments? What took you off track?

_____

_____

_____

Did you use your leftover time as you planned? How can you be more focused in the upcoming week?

_____

_____

_____

What one activity do you want to commit your leftover time to in the upcoming week?

_____

_____

Passion Point (Intrinsic Value)

If you had to spend $1,000 to improve one of your passions, how would you feel about it?

Would you be reluctant to make the improvement?

_____

_____

_____

_____

_____

_____

_____

_____

_____

_____

_____

_____

_____

_____

_____

_____

_____

_____

Chapter 8 Review

Adjusting Your Frequency

<u>Date</u>

Chapter Started: _____._____

Chapter Completed: _____

What information in the chapter
resonated with you?

Pages to revisit:

- Page:____
- Page:____
- Page:____
- Page:____
- Page:____
- Page:____
- Page:____
- Page:____

What are 3 insights that you learned or rediscovered about yourself?

Inspired Thoughts

_____

_____

_____

_____

_____

_____

_____

_____

_____

_____

_____

_____

_____

_____

_____

_____

_____

_____

_____

_____

_____

_____

BILLY F. WROE JR.

What's Happening?

Date: _____

What opportunities have you had to put into practice the information from this chapter? How have you been able to manifest your preferred outcome?

_____

_____

_____

_____

_____

_____

_____

_____

_____

_____

_____

_____

_____

_____

_____

_____

_____

_____

What's Happening?

Date: _____

What opportunities have you had to put into practice the information from this chapter? How have you been able to manifest your preferred outcome?

_____

_____

_____

_____

_____

_____

_____

_____

_____

_____

_____

_____

_____

_____

_____

_____

Free Flow Journal

Date: _____
Prompt: _____

_____

_____

_____

_____

_____

_____

_____

_____

_____

_____

_____

_____

_____

_____

_____

_____

_____

_____

_____

_____

_____

Free Flow Journal

Date: _____
Prompt: _____

_____
_____
_____
_____
_____
_____
_____
_____
_____
_____
_____
_____
_____
_____
_____
_____
_____
_____
_____
_____
_____
_____
_____

Timeout (What are You Attracting?)

Take the next 60 seconds to think about one thing that you recently attracted to yourself. Take the 1st thing that comes to mind, no matter how big or small it is. Now use the next 5 minutes to write down how you know that you attracted this to your life. Where were your thoughts? What actions led to its manifestation? Was the outcome positive or negative? Once you finish answering these questions, decide whether you want to attract more or less of this outcome in your life. What is one thing you can do in the next moment to increase or decrease the signal that you are receiving? Later when you have about 30 minutes do this same exercise again only using one of your passions as the attraction subject. Remember, there is an abundant signal waiting for you to tap into it.

<u>60-second Exercise:</u>

How can you increase or decrease the signal you are receiving?

_____

_____

_____

_____

_____

Timeout (What are You Attracting?)

Take the next 10 minutes to think about one passion that you are currently attracting to yourself. No matter how big or small, use a passion that you feel is significant to you. Now use the next 5 minutes to write down how you know that you attracted this to your life. What actions led to its manifestation? Was the outcome positive or negative? Once you finish answering these questions, use the next 15 mintues to decide whether you want to attract more or less of this outcome in your life. What is one thing you can do in the next moment to increase or decrease the signal that you are receiving? Remember, there is an abundant signal waiting for you to tap into it.

30-minute Exercise:

Attracted Passion:

How are your thoughts attracting or deflecting this passion?

_____

_____

_____

_____

Outcome

+   −

How are your actions helping to manifest this passion?

_____

_____

_____

_____

How can you increase or decrease the signal you are receiving to serve your passion?

_____

_____

_____

_____

_____

Passion Point (Regret Accountability)

Not being willing to admit our role in our greatest regrets, can cause them to haunt us for a lifetime. Accept accountability to make space for forgiveness.

What role did you play in your greatest regret?

_____

_____

_____

_____

_____

_____

_____

_____

_____

_____

_____

_____

_____

_____

_____

_____

Take a Moment (The Interviews)

Before we transition to the Now Hiring section, take a moment to reflect on your journey thru The Interviews. What foundational concept will be most helpful in supporting your passion? In what ways will it stabilize your passion? How can you appreciate yourself for sticking with your commitment? Answer these questions with as many one-word responses that you can. Then using those answers create a gratitude statement that acknowledges wisdom learned and refreshed.

What foundational concept will best support your passion? How?

What can you appreciate about making this journey?

Write a gratitude statement that encompasses that journey.

_____

_____

_____

_____

NOW HIRING

We all have a job posting open
for passion.

Chapter 9 Review

Create a True North

Date

Chapter Started: _____

Chapter Completed: _____

What information in the chapter
resonated with you?

Pages to revisit:

- Page:____
- Page:____
- Page:____
- Page:____
- Page:____
- Page:____
- Page:____
- Page:____

What are 3 insights that you learned or rediscovered about yourself?

Inspired Thoughts

_____

_____

_____

_____

_____

_____

_____

_____

_____

_____

_____

_____

_____

_____

_____

_____

_____

_____

_____

_____

_____

_____

_____

BILLY F. WROE JR.

What's Happening?

Date: _____

What opportunities have you had to put into practice the information from this chapter? How have you been able to manifest your preferred outcome?

_____

_____

_____

_____

_____

_____

_____

_____

_____

_____

_____

_____

_____

_____

_____

_____

_____

What's Happening?

Date: _____

What opportunities have you had to put into practice the information from this chapter? How have you been able to manifest your preferred outcome?

_____

_____

_____

_____

_____

_____

_____

_____

_____

_____

_____

_____

_____

_____

_____

_____

_____

Free Flow Journal

Date: _____
Prompt: _____

_____

_____

_____

_____

_____

_____

_____

_____

_____

_____

_____

_____

_____

_____

_____

_____

_____

_____

_____

_____

_____

Free Flow Journal

Date: _____
Prompt: _____

_____

_____

_____

_____

_____

_____

_____

_____

_____

_____

_____

_____

_____

_____

_____

_____

_____

_____

_____

_____

_____

_____

BILLY F. WROE JR.

Passion Point (True North)

When it comes to your passion, what is your truth?

What do you believe?

Where is that leading you?

_____

_____

_____

_____

_____

_____

_____

_____

_____

_____

_____

_____

_____

_____

_____

_____

Timeout (Toxic Truth)

Think about the truths that guide your identity. If you are a strong-willed person, you may believe that you cannot interact with hurt emotions, because strong people can't be hurt. If you are an empath and emotionally sensitive, you may not believe that strength is accessible to your identity. Where are you using these types of one-size-fits-all toxic truths in your life? Have some of these truths expired or did they never really exist in the first place?

Divide a piece of paper in half. On one side, take about 5-minutes to write what you feel are the most positive attributes about your identity. On the other side, take another 5-minutes to write what you feel are the most negative attributes about your identity. Once you have completed both sides, see if you can find any conflicting attributes. For example, if you were loving on your positive side, but indifferent on your negative side, those 2 attributes would conflict. Examine your conflicts and challenge yourself to decide if the attributes are true, conditionally true, or based upon a false/expired narrative. If you identify any conditional truths, work to become clearer on which conditions correlate to that truth and which do not. If you find false/expired narrative truths, work to debunk them, and rid your identity from the impact of their lies. I recommend going through this exercise at least once a year, but every 6 months is ideal.

Date: / /

Positive Attributes	Negative Attributes
1. _____	1. _____
2. _____	2. _____
3. _____	3. _____
4. _____	4. _____
5. _____	5. _____

BILLY F. WROE JR.

Conflicting Attributes (Note: an attribute can have multiple conflicting attributes)

_____ / _____   _____ / _____

Positive   Negative   Positive   Negative

_____ / _____   _____ / _____

Positive   Negative   Positive   Negative

Before continuing the exercise, set a calendar reminder to do this exercise again in 6 months. Be sure the event has a reminder for a week in advance, to give yourself time to intentionally shift your focus to your current state.

Next Exercise Date: ___/___/_____

Timeout (Toxic Truth)

Truth

Were any of your attributes true?   Do you desire for these
                                       attributes to remain true?

_____   _____

What is your strategy to reinforce or decommission those truths?

_____

_____

_____

Conditional Truth

Were any of your attributes conditionally true?

_____

What are the conditions in which these attributes exist?

_____

_____

_____

False Narrative

Were any of your attributes built upon a false narrative?

_____

What are the lies that you have opted to believe?

_____

_____

Timeout (Toxic Truth)

Think about the truths that guide your identity. If you are a strong-willed person, you may believe that you cannot interact with hurt emotions, because strong people can't be hurt. If you are an empath and emotionally sensitive, you may not believe that strength is accessible to your identity. Where are you using these types of one-size-fits-all toxic truths in your life? Have some of these truths expired or did they never really exist in the first place?

Divide a piece of paper in half. On one side, take about 5-minutes to write what you feel are the most positive attributes about your identity. On the other side, take another 5-minutes to write what you feel are the most negative attributes about your identity. Once you have completed both sides, see if you can find any conflicting attributes. For example, if you were loving on your positive side, but indifferent on your negative side, those 2 attributes would conflict. Examine your conflicts and challenge yourself to decide if the attributes are true, conditionally true, or based upon a false/expired narrative. If you identify any conditional truths, work to become clearer on which conditions correlate to that truth and which do not. If you find false/expired narrative truths, work to debunk them, and rid your identity from the impact of their lies. I recommend going through this exercise at least once a year, but every 6 months is ideal.

Date: / /

Positive Attributes   **Negative Attributes**

1. _____   1. _____
2. _____   2. _____
3. _____   3. _____
4. _____   4. _____
5. _____   5. _____

Conflicting Attributes (Note: an attribute can have multiple conflicting attributes)

_____ / _____		_____ / _____	
Positive	Negative	Positive	Negative
_____ / _____		_____ / _____	
Positive	Negative	Positive	Negative

Before continuing the exercise, set a calendar reminder to do this exercise again in 6 months. Be sure the event has a reminder for a week in advance, to give yourself time to intentionally shift your focus to your current state.

Next Exercise Date: ___/___/_____

Timeout (Toxic Truth)

Truth

Were any of your attributes true?

Do you desire for these attributes to remain true?

_____   _____

What is your strategy to reinforce or decommission those truths?

_____

_____

_____

Conditional Truth

Were any of your attributes conditionally true?

_____

What are the conditions in which these attributes exist?

_____

_____

_____

False Narrative

Were any of your attributes built upon a false narrative?

_____

What are the lies that you have opted to believe?

_____

_____

Chapter 10 Review

A Journey of 1,000 Steps

Date

Chapter Started: _____

Chapter Completed: _____

What information in the chapter
resonated with you?

Pages to revisit:

- Page:___
- Page:___
- Page:___
- Page:___
- Page:___
- Page:___
- Page:___
- Page:___

What are 3 insights that you learned or rediscovered about yourself?

Inspired Thoughts

_____

_____

_____

_____

_____

_____

_____

_____

_____

_____

_____

_____

_____

_____

_____

_____

_____

_____

_____

_____

_____

_____

What's Happening?

Date: _____

What opportunities have you had to put into practice the information from this chapter? How have you been able to manifest your preferred outcome?

_____

_____

_____

_____

_____

_____

_____

_____

_____

_____

_____

_____

_____

_____

_____

_____

_____

What's Happening?

Date: _____

What opportunities have you had to put into practice the information from this chapter? How have you been able to manifest your preferred outcome?

_____

_____

_____

_____

_____

_____

_____

_____

_____

_____

_____

_____

_____

_____

_____

_____

Free Flow Journal

Date: _____
Prompt: _____

_____

_____

_____

_____

_____

_____

_____

_____

_____

_____

_____

_____

_____

_____

_____

_____

_____

_____

_____

_____

_____

_____

_____

Free Flow Journal

Date: _____
Prompt: _____

_____

_____

_____

_____

_____

_____

_____

_____

_____

_____

_____

_____

_____

_____

_____

_____

_____

_____

_____

_____

_____

_____

Wisdom Quadrant

Relevancy

	Non Relevant	Memory Highlight
Short Term	You may or may not be able to access this information. To maintain access requires frequent repetition. Repetition keeps non relevant memories alive.	Fastest recall quadrant. Useful for knowledge-based solutions.
Long Term	Information is lost and must be reexperienced. Items can unintentionally fall into this category when we are distant from the present.	Deep wisdom, that we can recall from any distance. Makes up the core of many of our automated solutions.

Memory Term

How can you use your knowledge of how the Wisdom Quadrant functions to the advantage of your passion?

_____

_____

_____

_____

BILLY F. WROE JR.

Timeout (Does it Fit?)

The benefit of being able to see your passion sooner rather than later is that you can hold up ideas that you have about it ahead of time. Ask yourself if your present activities fit what you imagine your passion to be. In the boxes below, draw 4 different-sized triangles. In the 1st & 3rd triangles write the word "Passion". In the 2nd & 4th triangles write the word "Activities". Now match the 1st triangle with the 2nd, and the 3rd with the 4th. In your groups which triangle is larger, your passion or your activities? Does your passion fit into your activities? What needs to grow or shrink? Does a triangle need to be eliminated altogether? If you got lucky, on at least one of your activity triangles your passion triangle was able to fit with room for your passion to grow.

Triangle 1	Triangle 2

What needs to grow or shrink? _____

Why? _____

Triangle 3	Triangle 4

What needs to grow or shrink? _____

Why? _____

BILLY F. WROE JR.

Timeout (Does it Fit? - part 2)

Now let's repeat the triangle exercise. Knowing what you know about the importance of the triangle sizes, use something that you are actually passionate about in the 1st triangle. In the 2nd triangle write down a few of the activities you are doing to meet the needs of that passion Do those activities fit or does it look like you are rowing a boat in the middle of a desert? If your passion fits and has room for expansion, you are in a great position! If it feels like your passion is greater than your activities, explore where you see your passion going and either how you can incorporate more relevant activities, shrink the dimensions of your passion, or retire the passion altogether.

Triangle 1 (Passion)	Triangle 2 (Activities)

Which triangle you are going to change (circle one)?

Neither   Passion   Activities

How will the triangle be changed (circle one)?

Grow   Shrink   Eliminate

How will you implement the changes?

_____

_____

_____

_____

_____

BILLY F. WROE JR.

Chapter 11 Review

Challenge Impossibilities

Date

Chapter Started: _____

Chapter Completed: _____

What information in the chapter
resonated with you?

Pages to revisit:

- Page:____
- Page:____
- Page:____
- Page:____
- Page:____
- Page:____
- Page:____
- Page:____

What are 3 insights that you learned or rediscovered about yourself?

Inspired Thoughts

_____

_____

_____

_____

_____

_____

_____

_____

_____

_____

_____

_____

_____

_____

_____

_____

_____

_____

_____

_____

_____

_____

_____

What's Happening?

Date: _____

What opportunities have you had to put into practice the information from this chapter? How have you been able to manifest your preferred outcome?

_____

_____

_____

_____

_____

_____

_____

_____

_____

_____

_____

_____

_____

_____

_____

_____

_____

_____

What's Happening?

Date: _____

What opportunities have you had to put into practice the information from this chapter? How have you been able to manifest your preferred outcome?

_____

_____

_____

_____

_____

_____

_____

_____

_____

_____

_____

_____

_____

_____

_____

_____

_____

_____

BILLY F. WROE JR.

Free Flow Journal

Date: _____
Prompt: _____

_____

_____

_____

_____

_____

_____

_____

_____

_____

_____

_____

_____

_____

_____

_____

_____

_____

_____

_____

Free Flow Journal

Date: _____
Prompt: _____

_____

_____

_____

_____

_____

_____

_____

_____

_____

_____

_____

_____

_____

_____

_____

_____

_____

_____

_____

_____

_____

_____

Timeout (Keep Striving for Someday)

Besides his ability to regain mobility, there was one other thing that stood out to me about Arthur's story. He said, "Just because I can't do it today, doesn't mean that I can't do it someday." Take some time to think about a current impossible challenge in your life. List some of the symptoms that let you know it is there. Try to identify the actual issue. You may have tried to overcome this challenge multiple times to no avail but make a commitment to take a crack at it every opportunity you get the chance to. Though people may tell you that you are wasting your time, keep in mind that your limitations are yours to set and strongly based upon your beliefs. If today is not the day you achieve victory, continue to strive for someday. Review why you may have failed and determine if you were addressing the symptoms or the actual issue. Try to take the salvable pieces and create a new plan to address the issue. Most importantly don't be discouraged to try again. Repeat this exercise each time that you encounter a challenge that you fail to overcome. You will find that sometimes there are only little tweaks that need to be made, and other times you need a whole new approach. Remember that impossible is only impossible until it isn't.

The Impossible Challenge

Symptoms:

_____

_____

_____

Actual Issue

}

_____

Is this the actual issue?

Why did your last attempt to overcome the challenge fail?

_____

_____

_____

What adjustments can you make to better address the actual issue?

_____

_____

_____

Chapter 12 Review

An Unapologetic Pursuit

Date

Chapter Started: _____

Chapter Completed: _____

What information in the chapter
resonated with you?

Pages to revisit:

- Page:____
- Page:____
- Page:____
- Page:____
- Page:____
- Page:____
- Page:____
- Page:____

What are 3 insights that you learned or rediscovered about yourself?

Inspired Thoughts

BILLY F. WROE JR.

What's Happening?

Date: _____

What opportunities have you had to put into practice the information from this chapter? How have you been able to manifest your preferred outcome?

_____

_____

_____

_____

_____

_____

_____

_____

_____

_____

_____

_____

_____

_____

_____

_____

What's Happening?

Date: _____

What opportunities have you had to put into practice the information from this chapter? How have you been able to manifest your preferred outcome?

_____

_____

_____

_____

_____

_____

_____

_____

_____

_____

_____

_____

_____

_____

_____

_____

_____

_____

_____

Free Flow Journal

Date: _____
Prompt: _____

_____

_____

_____

_____

_____

_____

_____

_____

_____

_____

_____

_____

_____

_____

_____

_____

_____

_____

_____

_____

_____

_____

Free Flow Journal

Date: _____
Prompt: _____

_____

_____

_____

_____

_____

_____

_____

_____

_____

_____

_____

_____

_____

_____

_____

_____

_____

_____

_____

_____

_____

_____

Passion Point (Understanding the Blueprint)

Are you creating a Temporary Shelter or a Prison?

_____

_____

_____

_____

_____

_____

_____

_____

_____

_____

_____

_____

_____

_____

_____

_____

_____

_____

Chapter 13 Review

A Passion-Driven Life

Date

Chapter Started: _____

Chapter Completed: _____

What information in the chapter
resonated with you?

Pages to revisit:

- Page:____
- Page:____
- Page:____
- Page:____
- Page:____
- Page:____
- Page:____
- Page:____

What are 3 insights that you learned or rediscovered about yourself?

Inspired Thoughts

Take a Moment (Reflection)

Before we get into the final chapter of Fire Your Job, Hire Your Passion, I want you to take a moment to reflect on your journey up until this point. Do you remember where you began? How can you appreciate yourself for sticking with your commitment? Answer these questions with as many one-word responses that you can. Then using those answers create a gratitude statement that acknowledges wisdom learned and refreshed. Now let's finish strong!

Where did you begin (mentally, emotionally, intellectually)?

What can you appreciate about making this journey?

Write a gratitude statement that encompasses that journey.

_____

_____

_____

_____

What's Happening?

Date: _____

What opportunities have you had to put into practice the information from this chapter? How have you been able to manifest your preferred outcome?

_____

_____

_____

_____

_____

_____

_____

_____

_____

_____

_____

_____

_____

_____

_____

_____

What's Happening?

Date: _____

What opportunities have you had to put into practice the information from this chapter? How have you been able to manifest your preferred outcome?

_____

_____

_____

_____

_____

_____

_____

_____

_____

_____

_____

_____

_____

_____

_____

_____

_____

_____

Free Flow Journal

Date: _____
Prompt: _____

_____
_____
_____
_____
_____
_____
_____
_____
_____
_____
_____
_____
_____
_____
_____
_____
_____
_____
_____
_____
_____
_____
_____

Free Flow Journal

Date: _____
Prompt: _____

_____
_____
_____
_____
_____
_____
_____
_____
_____
_____
_____
_____
_____
_____
_____
_____
_____
_____
_____
_____
_____
_____

BILLY F. WROE JR.

Timeout (Embrace or Exile?)

Instructions

What type of people do you have in your tribe? Are those the people that will push you towards or chase you away from your passion? It is possible that we may like a person who is out of alignment with our long-term passion. If they are unwilling to come into alignment with our passion, as hurtful as it might be temporarily, we will have to choose what level of engagement we are going to allow them in our lives, if any at all.

Evaluate up to the top 10 people in your tribe and determine if they elevate your passion or take away from it. Write the top 3 attributes that each one brings into your life. If the attribute adds to the elevation of your passion, take a moment to express your appreciation for their support. If the attribute takes away from your passion, commit to having the difficult conversation about how they are out of alignment with your passion and decide if they are willing to become aligned. If they are not, you must make the decision as to how the relationship will proceed.

I understand how hard this exercise can be for you to complete, as I have had to have these conversations throughout the years with family members and current/former friends. I want to encourage you, that as challenging as these conversations can be, I have always come out on the other side of them better for it. The results were that I either removed opposition to my vision or gained deeper allyship with those closest to me. Whatever the outcome was, it truly turns out to be a win for both sides.

Relationships:

1. _____   6. _____

2. _____   7. _____

3. _____   8. _____

4. _____   9. _____

5. _____   10. _____

BILLY F. WROE JR.

Timeout (Embrace or Exile?)

Name: _____

Relationship: _____

Attributes   **Passion Impact**
                                          (Circle One)

1. _____   **+**   **−**
2. _____   **+**   **−**
3. _____   **+**   **−**

Relationship Result (Circle one):   **Embrace**   **Work to Align**   **Exile**

What date will you have the con-
versation about this relationship?   Initial once you have
                                                      had the conversation.

_____

Name: _____

Relationship: _____

Attributes   **Passion Impact**
                                          (Circle One)

1. _____   **+**   **−**
2. _____   **+**   **−**
3. _____   **+**   **−**

Relationship Result (Circle one):   **Embrace**   **Work to Align**   **Exile**

What date will you have the con-
versation about this relationship?   Initial once you have
                                                      had the conversation.

_____

Timeout (Embrace or Exile?)

Name: _____

Relationship: _____

<u>**Attributes**</u>   <u>**Passion Impact**</u>
                                                        (Circle One)

1. _____   **+**   **−**
2. _____   **+**   **−**
3. _____   **+**   **−**

Relationship Result (Circle one):   **Embrace**   **Work to Align**   **Exile**

What date will you have the con-
versation about this relationship?   ☐   Initial once you have
                                                had the conversation.

_____

Name: _____

Relationship: _____

<u>**Attributes**</u>   <u>**Passion Impact**</u>
                                                        (Circle One)

1. _____   **+**   **−**
2. _____   **+**   **−**
3. _____   **+**   **−**

Relationship Result (Circle one):   **Embrace**   **Work to Align**   **Exile**

What date will you have the con-
versation about this relationship?   ☐   Initial once you have
                                                had the conversation.

_____

Timeout (Embrace or Exile?)

Name: _____

Relationship: _____

Attributes

1. _____
2. _____
3. _____

Passion Impact
(Circle One)

+ **−**
+ **−**
+ **−**

Relationship Result (Circle one):   **Embrace**   **Work to Align**   **Exile**

What date will you have the conversation about this relationship?

_____

☐ Initial once you have had the conversation.

Name: _____

Relationship: _____

Attributes

1. _____
2. _____
3. _____

Passion Impact
(Circle One)

+ **−**
+ **−**
+ **−**

Relationship Result (Circle one):   **Embrace**   **Work to Align**   **Exile**

What date will you have the conversation about this relationship?

_____

☐ Initial once you have had the conversation.

Timeout (Embrace or Exile?)

Name: _____

Relationship: _____

Attributes   **Passion Impact**
(Circle One)

1. _____ **+** **–**
2. _____ **+** **–**
3. _____ **+** **–**

Relationship Result (Circle one): **Embrace**   **Work to Align**   **Exile**

What date will you have the conversation about this relationship?

☐ Initial once you have had the conversation.

_____

Name: _____

Relationship: _____

Attributes   **Passion Impact**
(Circle One)

1. _____ **+** **–**
2. _____ **+** **–**
3. _____ **+** **–**

Relationship Result (Circle one): **Embrace**   **Work to Align**   **Exile**

What date will you have the conversation about this relationship?

☐ Initial once you have had the conversation.

_____

Timeout (Embrace or Exile?)

Name: _____

Relationship: _____

Attributes

Passion Impact
(Circle One)

1. _____ **+**   **–**
2. _____ **+**   **–**
3. _____ **+**   **–**

Relationship Result (Circle one):   **Embrace**   **Work to Align**   **Exile**

What date will you have the conversation about this relationship?

_____

☐ Initial once you have had the conversation.

Name: _____

Relationship: _____

Attributes

Passion Impact
(Circle One)

1. _____ **+**   **–**
2. _____ **+**   **–**
3. _____ **+**   **–**

Relationship Result (Circle one):   **Embrace**   **Work to Align**   **Exile**

What date will you have the conversation about this relationship?

_____

☐ Initial once you have had the conversation.

Take Ownership

Date: _____

How are you going to solidify the experiences that you have shared over the course of reading this book? What commitment will you make to revisiting this journal in a future evolved state?

_____

_____

_____

_____

_____

_____

_____

_____

_____

_____

_____

_____

_____

_____

_____

_____

_____

_____

BILLY F. WROE JR.

Learn more about the 1stWroe at www.1stWroe.com

For booking details for Billy F. Wroe Jr, please
email bookings@1stWroe.com

Connect with us on: YouTube, IG, Facebook,
LinkedIn, & Twitter @1stWroe

CPSIA information can be obtained
at www.ICGtesting.com
Printed in the USA
LVHW081148220222
711704LV00003B/69